Wa

by Bill Fyfe Hendrie

Lang**Syne**
PUBLISHING
WRITING *to* REMEMBER

Lang**Syne**

PUBLISHING

WRITING *to* REMEMBER

79 Main Street, Newtongrange,
Midlothian EH22 4NA
Tel: 0131 344 0414   Fax: 0845 075 6085
E-mail: info@lang-syne.co.uk
www.langsyneshop.co.uk

Design by Dorothy Meikle
Printed by Printwell Ltd
© Lang Syne Publishers Ltd 2020

ISBN 978-1-85217-219-0

Wallace

SEPT NAMES:
None.

MOTTO:
For Liberty.

CREST:
Issuant from a crest coronet,
a dexter arm, in armour,
embowed, in hand a sword.

TERRITORY:
Ayrshire and Renfrewshire.

*"The spirit of the clan means much
to thousands of people"*

Chapter one:

The origins of
the clan system

by Rennie McOwan

**The original Scottish clans of the Highlands
and the great families of the Lowlands and
Borders were gatherings of families, relatives,
allies and neighbours for mutual protection
against rivals or invaders.**

Scotland experienced invasion from the
Vikings, the Romans and English armies from the
south. The Norman invasion of what is now
England also had an influence on land-holding in
Scotland. Some of these invaders stayed on and in
time became 'Scottish'.

The word clan derives from the Gaelic
language term 'clann', meaning children, and it
was first used many centuries ago as communities
were formed around tribal lands in glens and
mountain fastnesses.

The format of clans changed over the centuries, but at its best the chief and his family held the land on behalf of all, like trustees, and the ordinary clansmen and women believed they had a blood relationship with the founder of their clan.

There were two way duties and obligations. An inadequate chief could be deposed and replaced by someone of greater ability.

Clan people had an immense pride in race. Their relationship with the chief was like adult children to a father and they had a real dignity.

The concept of clanship is very old and a more feudal notion of authority gradually crept in.

Pictland, for instance, was divided into seven principalities ruled by feudal leaders who were the strongest and most charismatic leaders of their particular groups.

By the sixth century the 'British' kingdoms of Strathclyde, Lothian and Celtic Dalriada (Argyll) had emerged and Scotland, as one nation, began to take shape in the time of King Kenneth MacAlpin.

Some chiefs claimed descent from

ancient kings which may not have been accurate in every case.

By the twelfth and thirteenth centuries the clans and families were more strongly brought under the central control of Scottish monarchs.

Lands were awarded and administered more and more under royal favour, yet the power of the area clan chiefs was still very great.

The long wars to ensure Scotland's independence against the expansionist ideas of English monarchs extended the influence of some clans and reduced the lands of others.

Those who supported Scotland's greatest king, Robert the Bruce, were awarded the territories of the families who had opposed his claim to the Scottish throne.

In the Scottish Borders country – the notorious Debatable Lands – the great families built up a ferocious reputation for providing warlike men accustomed to raiding into England and occasionally fighting one another.

Chiefs had the power to dispense justice and to confiscate lands and clan warfare produced a society where martial virtues – courage, hardiness, tenacity – were greatly admired.

Gradually the relationship between the clans and the Crown became strained as Scottish monarchs became more orientated to life in the Lowlands and, on occasion, towards England.

The Highland clans spoke a different language, Gaelic, whereas the language of Lowland Scotland and the court was Scots and in more modern times, English.

Highlanders dressed differently, had different customs, and their wild mountain land sometimes seemed almost foreign to people living in the Lowlands.

It must be emphasised that Gaelic culture

was very rich and story-telling, poetry, piping, the clarsach (harp) and other music all flourished and were greatly respected.

Highland culture was different from other parts of Scotland but it was not inferior or less sophisticated.

Central Government, whether in London or Edinburgh, sometimes saw the Gaelic clans as a challenge to their authority and some sent expeditions into the Highlands and west to crush the power of the Lords of the Isles.

Nevertheless, when the eighteenth century Jacobite Risings came along the cause of the Stuarts was mainly supported by Highland clans.

The word Jacobite comes from the Latin for James – Jacobus. The Jacobites wanted to restore the exiled Stuarts to the throne of Britain.

The monarchies of Scotland and England became one in 1603 when King James VI of Scotland (1st of England) gained the English throne after Queen Elizabeth died.

The Union of Parliaments of Scotland and England, the Treaty of Union, took place in 1707.

Some Highland clans, of course, and Lowland families opposed the Jacobites and supported the incoming Hanoverians.

After the Jacobite cause finally went down at Culloden in 1746 a kind of ethnic cleansing took place. The power of the chiefs was curtailed. Tartan and the pipes were banned in law.

Many emigrated, some because they wanted to, some because they were evicted by force. In addition, many Highlanders left for the cities of the south to seek work.

Many of the clan lands became home to sheep and deer shooting estates.

But the warlike traditions of the clans and the great Lowland and Border families lived on, with their descendants fighting bravely for freedom in two world wars.

Remember the men from whence you came, says the Gaelic proverb, and to that could be added the role of many heroic women.

The spirit of the clan, of having roots, whether Highland or Lowland, means much to thousands of people.

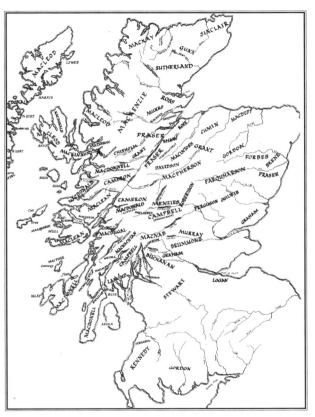

A map of the clans' homelands

Chapter two:

The real Braveheart

Sir William Wallace, Guardian of Scotland, has never been better known than now, thanks to all the publicity surrounding the film 'Braveheart'.

What, however, of the family of Wallace, whose name Scotland's greatest patriot so proudly bore?

It was during the so called peaceful Norman Conquest of Scotland in the reign of King David 1st that the Wallace family first came to Scotland. King David, who had been raised and educated at the English court, was eager to extend the benefits of the Norman influences of his youth to his homeland and so gave grants of land to many nobles from the south.

Among them was Walter Fitzalan, who the Scottish king appointed his steward in 1136 and it was as one of his followers that Richard Wallace from Oswestry came north to try and improve his fortunes along with those of his master. As Oswestry is on the Welsh border it seems possible that the name Wallace may be a corruption of Le Waleis or in other words, the Welshman.

From King David, Fitzalan received lands in Ayrshire and so it was in this part of Scotland that his follower Wallace also settled. Soon he too was granted an estate in Kyle, where it is claimed that his name Richard Wallace is still remembered in the placename of the village Riccarton.

Six generations later the Fitzalans still enjoyed the office of the steward to the Scottish monarch and when in 1316, Walter the Lord High Steward married Marjory, daughter of King Robert the Bruce it was the title of his office which gave the Scottish royal family the name of Stewart.

While the Fitzalans thus gained prominence in Scottish history, the Wallaces, who had followed them to the west of Scotland were also to achieve equal status in the history of our country, propelled to fame through the short but eventful life of their most prominent member, William.

William Wallace is believed to have been born in Elderslie, near Paisley, but the exact year of his birth is not certain. He was the second son of the Laird of Elderslie and Auchinbothie in Renfrewshire, Malcolm Wallace. While the Wallace family owned land, it was not a noble one. According to his earliest biographer, the poet Blind Harry, young Wallace was sent away from home to be educated at the monastery in Dunipace near Falkirk, where his uncle was one of the priests.

After completing his schooldays at Dunipace, Wallace continued his studies at Dundee, where he met John Blair, who later became his chaplain. It was to Blair that Blind Harry said he was indebted for most of his knowledge about Wallace as he recorded the facts of the patriot's life in Latin, a language in which Wallace himself was also proficient.

As a younger son, with no possibility of inheriting the family estate in Renfrewshire, it is possible that this education was designed to equip

William to follow down the nave in his uncle's footsteps, for a career in the church. Indeed his youth is described as a peaceful one, during which he worked hard at his lessons to perfect his knowledge of both Latin and French languages, which were to stand him in good stead during his exile from Scotlland, in the later part of his life.

There are two versions of how Wallace's peaceful studious life was suddenly shattered and he was propelled into the violent medieval world of Scottish politics. One is that while a student in Dundee he became involved in an incident with a young Englishman called Selby. Selby allegedly insulted Wallace, who in the resultant affray, struck and killed him. Wallace was as a result declared an outlaw by the English authorities in the Tayside city.

The other version is that the peaceful studious life of the youthful Wallace was shattered even more violently by another dramatic event, when his wife or lover, Marion Braidfute, was brutally raped and murdered by the hated English Sheriff of Lanark in May, 1297. After this he

Young Wallace drew a knife after being insulted by Selby

teamed up with other discontented young Scots including Sir John de Graham, Bishop Wishart of Glasgow and the Lord High Steward of Scotland, Sir Andrew Moray, who were already campaigning against the English overlords. Together Wallace and Moray became joint leaders of the Scottish resistance forces.

Amongst their daring exploits was an attack upon the English justiciar, Ormsby, while he was holding court at Scone near Perth. Ormsby succeeded in escaping, but many of his supporters were killed.

Wallace then heard that the English had murdered his uncle, Sir Ronald Crawford, and so led his ever growing band of resistance fighters south to Ayr, where they took their revenge by burning down the barracks of the occupying English forces.

When word of Wallace's deeds reached King Edward he ordered his army, under the command of Sir Robert Clifford and Sir Henry Percy to deal with him. The English caught up with Wallace and his Scottish fighters at Irvine.

Wallace was all for standing firm, but he was deserted by all of the other Scottish nobles, who vowed allegiance to Edward, apart from Sir Andrew Moray, who loyally stood by him.

In spite of being let down so badly by so many of his fellow Scots, Wallace rallied his remaining men and, marching north, was joined by many other supporters. With their help he regained most of the castles occupied by the English army north of the River Forth. In the late summer of 1297, he then returned to Dundee, where he had sufficient troops to besiege the city.

In the midst of the siege word reached him that a large English army was marching north to challenge him. Rather than wait, he marched his men south and took up position on the steep slopes of the rocky Abbey Craig on the north shore of the River Forth overlooking the vital strategic site of Stirling Bridge.

There on the 11th of September he challenged King Edward's hated English army to fight in the shadow of the famous castle. Wallace knew well that whoever held Stirling, held the keys to the Scottish kingdom.

Although the English troops were considerably superior in number, the Scots enjoyed the advantage of a superior position, high on the Abbey Craig, overlooking the winding River Forth, where the tall baronial tower of the Wallace Monument now marks the scene.

Approaching from the south east, the English army under John de Warenne, Earl of Surrey and Hugh de Cressington had the opportunity to cross the Forth, some distance down the river from Stirling at a shallow ford. Anxious to save time and put Wallace, Moray and their Scottish followers to the sword, Cressington insisted that his troops would cross direct using the narrow wooden Stirling Bridge. This they began doing shortly after dawn on that September morn.

Wallace and Moray held back their men until half the English soldiers, led by Cressington, were almost safely across the bridge. Then with bloodcurling shrieks they descended upon them. Penned in by the narrow sides of the bridge, there was no escape for the English enemy. Soon so many were slain that the bridge was blocked.

Their bodies prevented Salisbury from leading the other half of the English soldiers to join the fray. With Cressington already dead on the far shore of the river, Salisbury decided to retreat, leaving many of his English troops dead on the bridge.

In comparison, Scottish losses were light. Wallace pursued the vanquished English to Berwick, which he succeeded in capturing. From Berwick, Wallace led his followers south into Northumberland, both to harry the English and also to relieve pressure on supplies in the Scottish Borders. For a time they besieged the fortress at Newcastle from which the city took its name.

In the following spring, in the name of John Balliol, Wallace was proclaimed Guardian of Scotland, but already the English were gathering their troops to invade and reclaim what they regarded as their northern lands.

Chapter three:

From champion to martyr

Throughout the spring and early summer of the following year England's Edward I, The Hammer of the Scots, massed his troops, determined to have his revenge on Wallace. By the beginning of July his mighty army was encamped at Kirkliston, midway between Edinburgh and Linlithgow, to which his English fleet, moored in the River Forth off Queensferry, could provide much needed supplies.

Meanwhile Wallace too was preparing for the inevitable fray. High in the Bathgate Hills to the south of where Edward was positioned at Kirkliston, Wallace met with the Scottish nobles in the Preceptory at Torphicen. In this strange combination of church and castle, which still dominates the village to this day and which in his

Sir William Wallace

time was the headquarters of the Knights of St. John of Jerusalem, he held the last meeting of his Scottish parliament. From it one document with the great patriot's signature survives, ratifying a grant of land to a laird at Dundee.

As he met within the great thick stone walls of the Preceptory, Wallace received intelligence that Edward and his troops were moving forward to the Burgh muir on the flat ground to the east of Linlithgow Palace.

Next morning Wallace moved his men down the slopes of the Braes, the area to the south east of Falkirk and when Edward and the English enemy reached Polmont Muir the Scots leader was in a position ready to confront him.

Wallace had few horsemen compared with the English and what cavalry he had proved no match for the enemy. Wallace's infantry were therefore left totally exposed to bear the full onslaught of the flights of arrows fired by the deadly longbows of the English troops.

From high above the scene of the fighting, from the point still known as Wallacestone, where he had made his headquarters, the Scottish leader looked down on what was to become known as the Battle of Falkirk and knew that defeat was staring him in the face.

As hundreds of his men lay dying on the field below him, Wallace realised that he had not repeated the success of the year before at Stirling. Sadly the only choice left to him was to flee and seek refuge in the hope of fighting another day.

Despite the efforts of the English to capture him, Wallace managed to escape to the Continent, where he spent the next year trying to gather support and gain diplomatic recognition for Scotland. Thereafter Wallace returned in secret to Scotland and despite the dangers which he faced, managed to continue the campaign for independence for six more years.

In the end, however, he was betrayed in 1305 and captured at Robroyston near Glasgow. Wallace was taken to London for trial and eventual execution. In Westminster Hall, Sir William faced the obviously completely unjust charge of treason, as he had never recognised the authority of King Edward. The outcome was, however, inevitable. The Wallace was found guilty and sentenced not just to be put to death by public execution, but to suffer the indignity of being hanged then disemboweled while still alive and finally beheaded.

The terrible execution took place on the 25th of August, 1305, the English teasing out the whole dreadful business as a cat plays with a mouse. In the end, once Wallace was finally dead, they bloodthirstily dismembered his body and, once it was quartered, sent his four limbs back north, there to be displayed in Newcastle and Berwick-upon-Tweed and in Scotland itself at Perth and Stirling.

The work of stirring Scottish feelings of nationhood, which Wallace had so successfully begun was soon continued by Robert the Bruce. While the final victory over the English at Bannockburn in 1314 belonged to the Bruce, the tremendous contribution which Sir William Wallace made to the Scottish nationalist effort has never been forgotten. He is remembered not only by the national monument at Stirling, where a replica of his great two sided double bladed sword takes pride of place amongst the displays, but also by statues at St. Boswells in the Scottish Borders and at Elderslie, near Paisley, the place of his birth. Most appropriately, it is a statue of Wallace, by the sculptor, Alexander Carrick, which along with one of the Bruce, guards the gatehouse to Edinburgh Castle where it is spotlighted each August at the famous military tattoo.

Chapter four:

The Wallaces of Craigie

The Wallaces of Craigie from whom the senior branch of the family is descended obtained their estate during the early 17th century through marriage to the heiress of Sir John Lindsay of Craigie.

In 1669 Hugh Wallace of Craigie was one of the sons of Scottish nobility who was created a Baron of Nova Scotia under Sir William Alexander of Menstrie's scheme to promote that part of Canada as a Scottish colony.

On Hugh Wallace's death the leadership of the family passed to his grand nephew. He was the grandson of Hugh Wallace's brother, the Rev. William Wallace of Falford. The second Baronet was a lawyer and reached the height of becoming Lord Justice Clerk, the second highest judge in Scotland.

His son, the third Baronet, had no male heir and so the title went to his brother, who married another Wallace, the daughter of Sir Hew Wallace of Wolmet.

The fifth Baronet was Sir Thomas Wallace. His son, who was a captain in the Guards, died before him. In the middle of the 18th century the estates therefore passed to his daughter Frances, who married John Dunlop of Dunlop in Ayrshire, who was a friend of the poet Robert Burns.

Their heir adopted the name of Wallace, when he became the sixth Baron of Craigie. His attempt to maintain the family name was however in vain as he died without a direct heir and so representation passed to a cadet branch, the Wallaces of Cairnhill, who had for several generations been estate owners in the West Indies, in Jamaica. Through marriage the Wallaces of Cairnhill inherited the estates of Busbie and Clancaird.

In 1888 Captain Henry Wallace became clan chief. At the beginning of this century Robert Wallace of that Ilk was rewarded during the First World War with the French Crois De

Guerre. His son Malcolm also enjoyed a distinguished military career serving as a captain not only during the Second World War, but also during the 1950s in the Korean War and in the Far East in Borneo. He was chief of the Clan Wallace until 1991 when he was succeeded by his brother Ian, the 35th Wallace to hold that honour.

Among other modern Wallaces to gain distinction was the Scottish composer, William Wallace, who graduated from the University of Glasgow in 1885 and went on to enjoy a distinguished musical career, including writing the music for Maeterlinck's 'Pelleas and Melisande'.

Robert Wallace, the 19th century Member of Parliament, who was born in 1773 and died in 1855, was responsible for ensuring the passage through the House of the Act which turned Sir Roland Hill's idea for the penny post into relality in 1840.

Another Victorian of note was Alfred Russel Wallace, who independently put forward the same theories of evolution which brought much greater fame to Charles Darwin.

The editor of the tenth edition of the *Encyclopedia Britannica*, published in 1902, was Sir Donal MacKenzie Wallace.

After studying at both Glasgow and Edinburgh universities his early career included working as foreign correspondent for the *Times* newspaper, for whom he covered events in Egypt, Germany, Russia and Turkey.

Most famous of all, however, was Henry Agard Wallace, who was Roosevelt's choice as his Vice President of the United States of America in 1940. He went on to stand as a Presidential candidate in 1948 but was unsuccessful.

Leading branches of Clan Wallace in present day Scotland are the Wallaces of Cairnhill, the Wallaces of Cessnock, the Wallaces of Craigie, the Wallaces of Elderslie, the Wallaces of Kelly and the Wallaces of Riccarton.